A JEWISH DOCTOR IN AUSCHWITZ:
THE TESTIMONY OF SIMA VAISMAN

A JEWISH DOCTOR IN AUSCHWITZ:
THE TESTIMONY OF SIMA VAISMAN

INTRODUCTION BY SERGE KLARSFELD
FOREWORD BY DIANE VON FURSTENBERG

A JEWISH DOCTOR IN AUSCHWITZ:
THE TESTIMONY OF SIMA VAISMAN

INTRODUCTION BY SERGE KLARSFELD
FOREWORD BY DIANE VON FURSTENBERG

TRANSLATED BY CHARLOTTE MANDELL

MELVILLE HOUSE PUBLISHING
HOBOKEN, NEW JERSEY

©2005 Melville House Publishing

Originally published in French as:
Parmi les cris, un chant s'élève
Copyright 2002 Editions Michel Lafon

This work received support from the French Ministry of Foreign Affairs and
the Cultural Service of the French Embassy in the United States.

Melville House Publishing
P.O. Box 3278
Hoboken, NJ 07030
mhpbooks.com

Book design: David Konopka
Cover photo: © Michael St. Maur Sheil/CORBIS

ISBN: 0-9749609-9-3

Library of Congress Cataloging-in-Publication Data

Vaisman, Sima, 1903-1997.
  [Parmi les cris, un chant s'élève. English]
  A Jewish doctor in Auschwitz : the testimony of Sima Vaisman / by Sima Vaisman;
preface by Serge Klarsfeld ; afterword by Diane Von Furstenberg ;
translated by Charlotte Mandell.
       p. cm.
  Includes bibliographical references.
  ISBN 0-9749609-9-3
  1. Auschwitz (Concentration camp) 2. Vaisman, Sima, 1903-1997. 3. Jewish
physicians--France--Biography. 4. Holocaust, Jewish (1939-1945)--France--
Personal narratives. I. Title.
  D805.5.A96V3513 2005
  940.53'18'092--dc22

                                   2005003067

INTRODUCTION

Firsthand testimonies from strong personalities will always have more power to express the human authenticity of someone plunged into the world of concentration camps than even the most competent and best documentedwork of an historian.

So it is for the internment camps in France: no monograph on Le Vernet, Les Milles, Compiègne or Drancy can rival the force of the testimonies by Arthur Koestler[1], Lion Feuchtwanger[2], Jean-Jacques Bernard[3], Roger Gompel[4], Nissim Calef[5], Georges Wellers[6], François Montel or Georges Kohn[7].

Their works were written either during their imprisonment or after the Liberation. They had understood that, as firsthand witnesses, they had to bear witness, if they were able to—

either while they were still immersed in this extraordinary situation, or immediately after they had left this other planet onto which they had been cast.

This understanding, true for those interned in France, is valid too for the survivors of deportation. Of course, as deportees they were not in a position to bear witness while they were undergoing their terrible ordeals; but the most representative works of what the experience of a Nazi extermination camp was like for a Jewish man or woman were written or created soon after the Liberation. I would like to limit my examples to those who survived deportation from France.

Immediately upon returning, David Olère described the horror of what had happened in crematorium III in Birkenau in his "memorandum"— dozens of drawings of a photographic precision and, especially, his extremely precise diagram of the crematorium and the gas chamber.[8]

In 1945 Georges Wellers published his memorable *From Drancy to Auschwitz*, the work of a humanistic observer who, despite himself, was a participant in this inhuman experience.

Also in 1945 Yvonne Klug, whose story will soon be published, wrote with apparent detachment a brief and striking account of her deportation.

In 1999 I published the account that Xenia Gourvitch wrote in 1945 about her ordeals in Auschwitz. Dr. André

Leftich, deported from Angers on July 20, 1942, wrote upon his return *34 mois dans les camps de concentration nazis*, which relates, among other things, how during his thirty-four months in the concentration camps he took on the role of pathologist for the victims of Mengele's so-called medical experiments. Another work, published at the author's expense in 1945, was *Retour d'Auschwitz* (Return from Auschwitz) by Guy Kohen. Julien Unger's book, *Le Sang et l'Or* (Blood and Gold), which has a remarkable power, was published by Gallimard in 1946.

Another work written in the grip of immediate necessity was *Le Laminoir* by Serge Miller[9].

Some of these accounts did not produce much response or impact; life went on, and collectively we did not want to remember such tragedies. The surviving children of the exterminated deportees were still too young to impose their demand for remembering. That is why the terrible journey from Drancy to Auschwitz, the annihilation by gas of the large majority of the deportees, and the unspeakable sufferings endured by those picked for manual labor until almost all were slain—all these stories were pushed into the background of the preoccupations of a public memory more alert to the stories of the deportees of the Resistance than to those of a few surviving Jews, since the Resistance by that time was in control of the country. The memory of the Jewish deportees disappeared into the memories of the surviving members of their families and emerged only in ceremonies and reunions organized by the associations of deportees.

Fifteen to twenty years of silence ensued until new awareness of the fate of the Jews allowed the publication of new accounts by Jewish survivors; these were sometimes of great literary quality, but always less spontaneous, and thus containing less historic truth, than those that had been published immediately after the war.

None of these 1945 authors thought of themselves as writers. They wanted to be witnesses—not spectators passively present at some tragedy, but engaged witnesses since they themselves were victims. And for them it was less a question of testimony than of a deposition. They were not writing to justify themselves, but out of necessity: on the one hand personal necessity, to overcome through catharsis what they had survived and what had almost dehumanized them; on the other out of a collective necessity to give an account in the name of the others, the ones who had not survived and who had passed on their memories to them, their repositories.

None of these authors had to cope with the loss of their parents, spouses, or children; this allowed them to observe even before giving an account, since they had been saved from the worst of sufferings, the one that strikes your deepest love and makes you indifferent to the outer world.

All these witnesses benefited from a good education and a curious, attentive mind. Some were doctors, chemists; Olère was a painter.

Sima Vaisman, whose account appears here in a new edition, also responded, immediately upon returning, to this psychological and moral imperative, whose result was that these works by a few witnesses were the immediate extension of their deportation, rather than the fruit of an effort of memory required by the passage of time, the composition requires the use of flashbacks.

I knew Sima Vaisman, who practiced as a dental surgeon across the street from my home and whom my mother, also a Russian, used to visit. As director of *Le Monde juif*, the journal of the CDJC (Centre de Documentation Juive Contemporaine), in 1990 I published her account, written in the summer of 1945, as soon as I saw it, so important did it seem to me.[10]

Sima describes the Birkenau camp with such precision—though she could not have seen a map of it and saw only what was in her field of vision—that I have included with her text a map and notes, some of which are mine but most of which are by Jean-Claude Pressac, a specialist in the Auschwitz-Birkenau camp and in the functioning of the gas chambers and crematorium furnaces.[11]

Sima's text deserves, despite its brevity, to be published as a book, since it so concisely reveals the conditions of the extermination of the Jews in this slaughterhouse that was Birkenau. Not only does Sima know how to explain how the concentration camp system functions, but her descriptions are haunting and unforgettable, perhaps because she makes an abstraction of herself. She is there like a camera, but one that is not impartial—it has taken sides, because it is guided by an eye that is full of humanity. No one has told, as she has done, of the scenes of delousing or selection for the gas chamber in the so-called hospital, the *Revier*, and the transportation of the condemned to their death. In 1980, I had found *The Auschwitz Album* and its two hundred photographs; Sima in some way had already written the captions for the photographs of those "unfit for work," of that "living lava" pouring onto the crematoria: "Sometimes under the driving rain, sometimes under a burning sun, pass, stream, floods of people, young women with children in their arms, women who on the way are still giving their breast full of life, full of sap, to keep their babies from crying. Their skirts are clutched by the little children who already know how to walk, superb children, brown-haired and blond, with their curls floating on the breeze...."

Sima tells how in 1944 the prisoners, among them mothers who had outlived their children, prepared toys and Christmas gifts for the children of Germany with the toys and clothes of murdered Jewish children. She also describes the bloody evacuation of the camps that annihilated the great majority of the survivors forced on death marches.

No reporter in the world could have related, as Sima Vaisman has done in eighty pages, in a hundred thousand characters, what this Hell was like that the Jews experienced on Earth. No reporter, no novelist, no historian—only a witness, one of the earliest....

—SERGE KLARSFELD

FOREWORD

Sima Vaisman and my father, Lipa (Leon) Halfin, were first cousins. Their mothers were sisters and they lived in the same house in Kishinev, Bessarabia (now Moldova).

Sima's mother, Genia, was a widow. And my grandmother Sarah asked her husband, a well-to-do merchant, to welcome the mother and daughter to live with them. It was a large house with a beautiful garden where the other four sisters of Sarah and Genia and their families would celebrate holidays and birthdays. Genia was considered the wise one in the family, and Sima took after her.

Sima studied medicine in Bucharest, and became a doctor. In the 1930's she left Bessarabia, married, and, fleeing the increasing persecution of the Jews in Romania, she moved to Paris. There, lacking the means to get further medical degrees, she became a dental surgeon.

Meanwhile, my father, at the age of 18, also left Bessarabia. He went to Belgium to join his brother who was at university there. His brother returned home after graduation; my father never graduated and never went back. His father had died, the family business had been sold, and his mother urged him to stay in Belgium.

During the war, Sima fled to Lyon and was eventually arrested by the Germans in Mâcon in 1942. She was deported to several camps before arriving at Auschwitz and later she was transferred to Ravensbrück.

In the camps, she was assigned to the "hospital" and was relatively protected. There, she met a young girl from Belgium, Lily. They liked each other. Lily was reserved and never told Sima that she knew someone from Bessarabia, a handsome young man she had fallen in love with. Had she done that, Sima would have known it was her cousin Leon.

The war ended and—miraculously—both Lily and Sima survived. Back in Belgium, Lily married Leon and soon after I was born.

When my father took my mother to Paris to meet his cousin, the two women recognized each other. What happened?

I don't know. Neither of them were very talkative on the subject of the camps. Between them, there was almost a silent complicity... the camps were not a favorite subject.

As a child, growing up in Belgium, I remember my father calling cousin Sima on the telephone and speaking endlessly in Russian whenever he had an important decision to make.... "She is the wise one," he would say.

That is how I remember Sima—wise, pragmatic, detached and able to dissect any problem, any situation. Like her mother, she had become a widow, living alone and seeing her patients. She read a lot, supervised the education of her nieces and kept in touch with all the members of the family who had survived the war. I did not see her often, but her closeness to my father, and the fact that she was, for him, such a symbol of strength, justice and wisdom, made her nonetheless a presence.

Sima's tale of the camps is strong, gripping, often hard to read or believe. She had written it eight days after being freed by the Russians, as if to bury it somewhere and never have to think about it again. And it is the only such account by a female doctor.

My cousin, her niece Eliane Neiman-Scalie, discovered the manuscript by chance, in 1983. Sima brushed it aside, saying it was "of no interest," but she allowed Eliane to read it and to later publish it. But she did not want to talk about it much herself. Like my mother when asked about her experience in the camps, she did not want to talk about the misery and the atrocities, but rather about the friendships and the hope that somehow allowed them to survive the impossible.

This text is written in her voice—a voice of intelligence, detachment (how else?) and disgust ... the voice of a survivor. It is my duty and honor to help it be published in English ... in the name of Sima, of my mother, and of all those who perished.

—DIANE VON FURSTENBERG

PREFACE

TO THE FIRST EDITION OF SIMA VAISMAN'S TEXT
PUBLISHED IN THE JOURNAL *LE MONDE JUIF*, 1945

We are publishing below the deposition of a Jewish dentist deported from France. Originally from Bessarabia, Sima Vaisman was forty-one years old when she became part of convoy No. 66 on January 20, 1944, destination Auschwitz-Birkenau. She had been arrested with false papers in the name of Simone Vidal. A dentist by profession, she did not have the right to practice, under the racist laws of Vichy.

Sima Vaisman's account was written immediately upon her return from the camps, for fear of losing the precise memory of the events and places she had encountered. It is of a genuine historic interest and contains much precious information, because of its author's acute sense of observation and because of the scientific training she had received.

The notes that comment on and confirm what is related in this text were written by the editors of *Le Monde juif*.[12]

A JEWISH DOCTOR IN AUSCHWITZ:
THE TESTIMONY OF SIMA VAISMAN

Arrested in Saône-et-Loire on December 23, 1943 by the Feldgendarmerie of Mâcon, taken to the Gestapo in Lyon, I stayed a little while in this city in the prison of Montluc. Transferred to Drancy, after a few weeks spent in the camp's prison, I was placed in the deportation section and, on January 20, 1944, under the protective gaze of French gendarmes, after having heard a short speech from the director promising us that we would be going to labor camps where families would not be separated, where the old would do household chores, where only the young would work the hardest (everyone of course in his own profession), they put us on buses and brought us to the train station.

Summarily counted by German soldiers, our hearts heavy as lead, we numbered 1,200;[13] we entered the cattle cars, prepared for us in advance: 60 people per car, men, women, and children crammed together; on the ground a few dirty straw mattresses, a tin chamber pot, a bucket of water... The doors to the cars are sealed; we settle ourselves in the dark as best we can and the journey to the unknown begins.

Will we stop in Metz? Will there still be a sorting out there (one of the promises of the camp directors)? The train goes on without stopping all day, all night, we must have passed the French border a long time ago, the can fills up... the supply of water diminishes.

The train stops... starts again... we know nothing, hear nothing.

At the end of the second day, some of us receive permission to leave the car under escort and go to a river that is flowing at the base of a gravel slope to fill our can of water. Dirty water that is drinkable, the S.S. tell us.

We are in Germany. After a few minutes, we are put back in the cars and the journey begins again. Where? None of us knows.

On the third day, a guard comes to tell us that we have to give him a certain quantity of cigarettes for the "French prisoners," or else... he'll come search us and take them himself.

At the next stop, he comes to get them and tells us in confidence that they are taking us to Auschwitz in Upper Silesia.

Auschwitz, land of death.... The "die of fate" is cast, we must submit to it and hold strong, hold strong above all.

No more water, the chamber pot overflows, the people sitting around it are constantly being splashed. We try, through the gap in the doors (on the third day the doorways were sealed only by chains), to reason with the guards to let us at least empty the can, to take on a little water in a train station. Nothing to be done, they do not listen to us. Morale ebbs away. The people, dirty, tired and dying of thirst, impatiently await the arrival at the camp.

Around eleven in the evening the train stops. We have arrived. The journey has lasted three days and two nights.[14]

At midnight, they order us to get out.[15] The S.S. immediately separate the women and children from the men, snatch our packages, our suitcases, our bags from us, line us up in rows. We flounder in the mud. Shadows in "pajamas" (these are the camp detainees forced to work at the station) climb up behind us into the cars, take away everything that's still there, and load up some trucks with our suitcases and belongings.

An S.S. officer passes by and asks the doctors to step out of the rows, then calls for single women without families. Should I step out? Wouldn't it be better to join the families and stay with one's friends? Didn't they formally promise us an easier life, a lighter kind of work in "family camps"? Some of us make up our minds, leave the rows. Some S.S. aim the beam of their flashlights at them, even though the station is lit up by floodlights.

They choose the young, the ones in good health. There are 40 of us women who have to follow the S.S., out of the 700 women and children of the convoy.

The others climb into trucks and are brought directly to the crematorium, into the gas chambers....

We learn later on that the number of men who entered the camp is about the same as ours; of them 5% survived.... They take us to the camp, to the "sauna"[16] (the baths) under an S.S. escort. There, we are received by sleepy, fat, vulgar girls, still young, but looking pregnant (a common deformity among the detainees). On their left sleeve a registration number is sewn.

It is these girls, these detainees, who undress us, search us, tattoo us, take off our rings, our watches, our bags, don't even let us keep a toothbrush, a piece of soap, not even a photograph, shave off our hair and send us completely naked into the shower.

After the shower (no towel), we go into a large cold room, ice-cold, with a cement floor, where other girls hand out to us those poor rags that will henceforth have to serve as our clothes, rags to wrap our feet in, old worn-out shoes that are too small or too big. They paint red crosses on these miserable clothes, symbol of this heavy cross we will have to bear.

Thus disguised, unrecognizable, we go into an office where they register us, ask our profession, what studies we've completed, if we are sick, the number of gold teeth we have (for later recuperation, after death, natural or by gas).

We are ready.... Our slave existence begins.

In Birkenau, the blocks[17] where the detainees live are made of large bricks (made with the ashes of those incinerated,[18] we are told by the prisoners who have been there for a long time and who built this camp themselves).

Inside, the floor is made of red bricks. On either side of a short, narrow hallway, two passageways, on both sides of which sorts of rabbit cages face each other in three rows, one on top of the other. I can find no expression more appropriate to designate our future beds than that of "rabbit cage." Each cage is 6 x 3 feet (the size of a body). There are six of us in a cage. We are forced to sleep head-to-foot. We can also sit up but only by bending over, since the cages are low.

We are received in this block by girls just as fat and coarse, who only know how to shout and hit, and who literally terrorize us.

These girls, who are prisoners themselves, make up the administration of the block: the *stubovas*,[19] that's to say the ones in charge of cleaning, and the *blocova*, the woman director. The personnel are appointed by the camp S.S., who know very well how to choose the "best," meaning the ones who serve them better than they could themselves—the ones who know how to walk over corpses. They are for the most part Slovak and Polish women.

We spend entire days in these "cages," sitting completely bent over (we do not have the right to stretch out during the day). They just make us get out to do the work of the *stubovas* for them, for these "ladies" claim they have worked and suffered enough in the camp. All these former detainees think we have profited from life while they were locked up, so that it's our turn to work.

When they feel like it, they accompany us to the toilet where we go in rows. There, other Polish women also beat us with sticks, for we don't dare sit down on the wet, dirty boards.

Diarrhea is rampant. So much the worse for the ones who can't keep it in—they just have to take off their only pair of underpants.

Our food is distributed to us by these same *stubovas* who, in front of us, search through the soup pots to pick out the few pieces of potato or the tiny pieces of meat that might be floating in it, serve themselves copiously and leave us the rest. A dirty, grey, thick soup, without salt, absolutely inedible, served in a kind of wide metal mess tin. One mess bowl for six, and no spoon. We will have to "organize" ourselves, the old ones tell us, that means steal from our neighbor or, if we can, "buy" with our poor ration of bread from a more starving detainee.

After a few days they bring us to work: this consists of building the road; we have to do excavation work, or walk two and a half miles in both directions six or seven times a day, on foot, each time carrying a stone. We are accompanied by S.S. followed by police dogs who hurl themselves at those of us who can no longer walk and tear them to pieces. That amuses our S.S. a lot. The cries of the wretched women make them laugh.

In short we lead a well-regulated life in camp. Up at four every morning. We make our "beds," which means we carefully arrange "our" straw mattresses in rows (two mattresses for six people), we fold our blankets, for we have "blankets" too, dirty, stinking rags, one for two people. They chase us out of the block at 4:30 and, no matter what the weather, those interminable roll-calls begin.

In rows of five, without moving, we wait for hours in the snow and mud until the time the German S.S. deigns to come count us. Beware, those who dare say a word, move about, or don't stand at attention when the S.S. passes. Beware, too, those who faint. At the summons, everyone must be present and standing. We hold up the ones who fall from exhaustion, so that the S.S. won't see them on the ground. We revive them any way we can when roll-call is over.

After roll-call, it's work time. Soup is brought to us at noon, outside, if we are far from the blocks. When we work inside the camp, we return to the block for an hour.

At one o'clock we go back to work and go on till six or seven in the evening. It depends on the season. After work, it's roll-call again, more hours standing, and finally we return to the block where they distribute to us, not the ration we are entitled to (bread and 20 grams of margarine, three times a week) or sausage (one link) two times a week or a spoonful of beet jam twice a week, but this reduced ration, because the block personnel want to eat their fill, so they exchange for food what they steal from our poor ration of cigarettes, "clothes," etc.

We have to go outside again to take our shoes off (half an hour of standing up) since the block must always be clean inside and, when we have finally penetrated into this "sanctuary," we climb as quickly as possible into our "cages." We hide the remnants of our bread, if we have any, and our dirty shoes under the mattress, since otherwise everything would be stolen from us during the night. Without undressing, our clothes often still wet, rags on our heads, rubbing against each other, forced, since there's no room, to turn over as soon as one of us turns over, we try to fall asleep in this stinking block. At night they place, in the middle of the block, a bucket that two of us are supposed to empty in the morning, since we don't have the right to leave the block to relieve ourselves, and most of us have diarrhea. Scarcely have we fallen asleep than the night guard (*stubova*) begins to shout "get up," "make your beds," and her words are followed by blows; various objects (brushes, brooms, mess kits) are thrown into the upper levels when she notices someone who hasn't immediately gotten up.

The bravest manage to slip outside unseen, run to the toilet where they try to clear a place for themselves near the only faucet in the camp where one can wash up a little. There are about 12,000 of us in the camp where there are only two faucets.[20]

And another day similar to the ones before begins, sad, interminable, hopeless, in filth and shameful lack of privacy.

Many of us cannot bear these humiliations, this life, and throw ourselves on the electrified barbed wire fence that surrounds the camp. That is the only way to commit suicide.

One fine day, three weeks after my arrival in the camp, they come to call me to the *Revier*, the sick-bay.[21] Typhus is raging,[22] many doctors are already dead, some still sick, they need reinforcements.

The *Revier* is made up of a group of wooden barracks (ex-stables, as the inscriptions still on the doors indicate). There are fifteen barracks in all, of which eleven are used for different wards: the contagious, surgery, edemas, convalescents, dysentery, tuberculosis, general medicine; one barracks is reserved for the sick German prisoners, one for the staff, and two for consultations, for the kitchen and the annexes. The whole is surrounded by a barbed wire fence. The barracks are wood, old, black, the floor in some of them is brick, in some others, earth, in the middle there is a brick stove that they light from time to time. At both ends a large door (gate) that leads directly outside. No water, no plumbing. Light penetrates through little skylights in the ceiling. Inside, against each wall length-wise, beds (what an irony to call them that) placed end to end. Perpendicular to them, groups of two beds separated by a little space. Black, dirty cots in three tiers. A repugnant straw mattress full of pus and blood with one or two blankets, and on each mattress at least two sick people, sometimes even three or four. From time to time a bed on top collapses... cries, lamentations... and everything again returns to order. Near the beds, in the central row of cots, a few cans that the "nurses" empty from time to time. A smell of corpses, of excrement.... And the sick, skeletal beings, almost all covered with scabies, boils, devoured by lice, all completely naked, shivering from cold under their disgusting covers. Their shaved heads strangely resemble each other. These figures of suffering, ageless, are all the same. I spend weeks trying to get accustomed to them, trying to distinguish one from the other.

The "nurses," most of them well-nourished girls, in good health, who steal from the sick and rarely deign to approach them out of fear of being forced to render them a service, wash the floor all day, since the bricks must be constantly moist so that the S.S. get the impression of a clean block. What does it matter that the sick person is dirty, ill cared-for, full of lice and scabies, so long as appearances are saved?

I am drafted into Block 18 (general medicine).[23] The emaciated, the tuberculars, the typhoid victims, the ones swollen with hunger edema, or thrombophlebitis, with dysentery, or malaria, endlessly pass before us.

It should be noted that in general the deportees no longer have their periods.

The death rate is enormous. The *Revier* has 3,000 or 4,000 sick out of 12,000 to 13,000 detainees.[24] In the *Revier* alone, 300 die daily, the majority from typhus. The dead are dragged from the bed where they often spent a night next to another comrade in misery still alive, sometimes their mother or their sister, and thrown outside the block, naked of course, into the mud or the snow according to the season, for it is rarely dry in this swampy country. There the piles rapidly grow. Surreal vision of these little mountains of dead bodies, covered with one single cover. Legs, arms, faces of suffering jut out on every side....

In the evening, a truck arrives and loads its lugubrious cargo to carry it to the crematoriums that smoke without stop. And new corpses are piled up... still the factory of death continues to operate. And can it be any other way? We have a hospital, we have medical personnel, but they do not give us any medicine; no cotton, no gauze, nothing with which to make a bandage. What they do give us is so minimal that we can consider it almost nonexistent. Whether it's for the service of infections, of edemas, or of dysentery, every day they send us the same thing:[25] ten aspirin tablets, ten charcoal tablets, ten tablets of urotropine, ten tablets of Tamalbrul, occasionally a syringe of cardiazol, of caffeine, or of Prontosil; a little cellulose cotton and paper strips once a week, with which to make temporary bandages, for the most urgent cases. And all those abscesses that open by themselves! The pus runs onto the patient, onto the covers; these innumerable beings with frozen feet, with gangrene, writhing with pain, beg you to give them a little cotton, a tablet to calm the suffering... with their faces of suffering, all the same, they impatiently await our visits, their eyes follow us and beg us in their bodies devoured by scabies, they use their tiny bit of margarine, rub themselves to try to calm their tortured skin....

We can only give them a kind word or, if by chance we get a few things from the pharmacy (one day, for instance, kilos of kaolin), we give them kaolin for dysentery, kaolin for entero-colitis, kaolin to take care of their (external) scabies.

When we get hold of a few tablets of Solvens, we prepare a solution of it and the sick swallow this poor spoonful of "blessed water," as we call it, with so much confidence that they "feel" immediately relieved. And we can only give it to the women with tuberculosis, or to those with bronchitis, but from all the beds hands stretch out, poor voices beg to be granted a little of this "blessed water" and, when we tell them it's only for the ones coughing, they reply that they're also coughing... which is true, unfortunately. The number of tubercular cases is large.

It was in November 1943[26] that the struggle began in the *Revier* and in the camp against lice but, upon my arrival in February 1944, the sick were always covered with them, and typhus raged....

We make our visits with scarves on our heads. When we lean over a sick woman, lice fall onto our heads from the upper bunks. And the de-lousing was still one of the atrocious things in the camp. It was done block by block. Everyone was sent to the "sauna"[27] (the bath house), the sick from the *Revier* as well as those not sick. The dying women were carried on stretchers, the others, that's to say all those who could still stand upright, had to go there by foot (a distance of about a quarter of a mile). Naked, shirtless, feet wrapped in worn-out slippers, covered with a meager blanket, often two under one blanket which covered only their chest. Their long fleshless thighs don't touch each other, and leave enormous triangles between them. Their long legs (two thin sticks covered with a parchment skin) give way to enormous knees. They drag themselves lamentably in the snow (at times it was as cold as -15 degrees Fahrenheit) or in the mud, fall on the way, get back up under blows from batons, drag themselves again. Faces dried up, triangular, ageless, in which only the eyes could be seen, were twisted in suffering. They shaved the ones who had head lice (and almost all of them did), showered them. Sitting on the cement floor, they waited for hours, often all night, for the blankets to be disinfected (passed under the sterilizer) and the block gassed. That day, quite often, their soup was not distributed to them either....

On the way back, they brought the dead on stretchers. The death rate after this de-lousing was enormous, the disinfection insufficient, and the lice continued to devour our sick. However, their number was diminishing.

Around April 1944, the de-lousing was done differently in the *Revier*. They transferred the sick to be de-loused into another block of the *Revier* for one day, still on foot, still naked, still under blows. This block already had its sick, whom they put in threes and fours into one bed to make room for the "guests."

These "guests" were also bedded in threes and fours. They had phlegmons, abscesses, frozen feet, uncontrollable diarrhea (the sick would just do it where they lay), typhus, scabies, all piled up pell-mell, no matter how, on top of each other. The beds continually collapsed, the sick from the upper bunks fell onto their comrades in misery below injuring themselves, injuring them. No blanket for the "guests," since the blankets had to remain in the block that was being gassed.

The next day, they shaved the sick and "washed" them. No water in the blocks, no plumbing. So they brought in a bathtub and poured a few jugs of water into it. Occasionally they'd throw in a few crystals of potassium permanganate[28] (when the pharmacy had some) and the 350 or 400 sick women to be de-loused were all soaked, "washed" in the same water that became black and thick with grime. They took off the bandages (couldn't the lice be living underneath?) and the pus poured into the bathtub. The ones who still had a relatively clean body still had to enter the bathtub, the sick ones lying down were soaked with it.... And again they returned to their "clean" block, again they brought out the living corpses that they threw onto the piles in front of the block (after having taken down the registration number on their arms).

But when the number of survivors of the *Revier* was great, they made "selections" from time to time, in order to keep from feeding all these useless mouths.

Suddenly, in the middle of the day, the order came to close all the blocks, to let no one out. They shot at the ones who dared to try to leave.

A commission made up of the head S.S. doctor of the hospital, a few S.S. officers, and our main doctor (woman director), who was a detainee, went into one block after another. Everyone already knew what was going to happen. An enormous panic spread among the Jewish patients. The word *Sortierung* (selection) ran from one mouth to the other. They would have risked everything and tried to run outside, to hide somewhere in a ravine, but they were naked and would have been spotted immediately.

The personnel of the block (the medical staff was not subject to these selections) started to take out all their things, to help dress at least a few. But, none of us had much to put on. Repeated searches had deprived us of a pullover, or a skirt, or a shirt we might have contrived to "organize." We had a right only to what we had on, no change of underwear, no dress. We quickly distribute our coats, our blouses, our aprons. All the sick throw themselves on us, literally tear our clothes from us, beg us to give them a few rags. And the ones who no longer had any strength, could almost no longer move, still braced themselves, and got up; they were the ones who often snatched most fiercely at our clothes.

The few patients who had transformed themselves in this way into "nurses" pretend to wash, to massage the sick, and to hide, as much as they can, their anxious faces from the searching eyes of our executioners.

Others try to hide themselves between the beds, to slip under the beds... but the beds are barely 10 inches high and even though they're just skin and bone, in vain they try to slip under the beds; we pull out stuck bodies (their backs all torn and cut up), people with wandering gazes, with mad eyes.

And the commission is already there.... A silence of death.... No one dares to breathe. Everyone gets out of the beds and goes to one side of the block. All the beds, all the spaces between each gap where a poor body might have hidden itself, are verified by the S.S., baton in hand. Blows rain down on those they find, their numbers are recorded, their death warrant is signed... This happens also to all the women who, having no more strength left, despite all their will, cannot get out of bed. And the sinister procession begins in front of the commission.

They go, one by one, from one side of the block to the other. They gather their last remaining strength, they brace themselves in order not to stumble. These ageless faces, these faces of suffering, crease into a grimace they think is a smile, to hide their suffering, to seem brave still.

Cold and impassive, with an expression of disgust, the S.S. doctor makes a slight sign of the hand: to the left or to the right. To the left, the numbers are recorded, the death warrant is signed, no hope for a reprieve. And those who escape these selections are few. They are, for the most part, the most recent arrivals in the camp who, still having a clean body (no scabies, or wounds, or abscesses), have preserved some female allure. But these "doctors" were "aesthetes" and kept only pretty bodies. One of our friends, the wife of a Dutch poet, young and one of the most beautiful women in the camp, would be among the condemned. She had given birth in a camp in Holland, just before her deportation, and had a few stretch marks on her belly.

In the block there are also Aryans, a mixed block as it was called (for there was also a block only of Jews); the lists of Jews were drawn up rapidly at the hospital secretariat, so they alone came out and filed in front of the commission.

Their lugubrious duty accomplished, as impassive as at their arrival speaking about commonplace things amongst themselves, the S..S. withdrew. Their work had lasted just a few minutes. The joy of some, the tortures of others, had only just begun.

Cries, tears, lamentations, prayers.... Everyone shows her suffering in her own way. The "spared" ones embrace each other, vent their joy at the top of their voices, but they still have wandering gazes, mad looks.... They know that their turn too will come and probably soon, but today they have won the "jackpot," a few days more, a few weeks or maybe even a few months of torture, misery, life of martyrdom! Isn't that some luck? What does the suffering of the others matter.... Life in the camp has already taught them to care only for themselves, to step indifferently, unfeelingly, past the greatest suffering!

The selection over, the administration of the *Revier*, made up of us detainees, enters the scene. It separates those condemned to death from the others, the survivors.

One of the blocks, normally the Jewish block, is transformed for a few days into an enormous cell of those condemned to death (from 350 to 600 sometimes). The block is surrounded; no one, except the personnel of the block, has the right to enter it. The *blocova* is responsible for the number of those "selected." If someone escapes, one of the women of the personnel will have to take her place. It's not the person that counts, it's the number....

And this strange life, unreal in its monstrosity, begins.

Cases of madness multiply. One woman cries out, the other shouts, gnaws her arms, one speaks softly, with a smile that is no longer of this world, to her little girl, her little Mariette whom she sees playing next to her. Another is impassive, resigned. One of my friends tells me with a celestial smile not to go to too much trouble for her, that she is happy to die, since she has just learned that her husband is dead like her and she wants to hurry to rejoin him... and her daughter, her little two-year-old girl who stayed hidden with friends, is so sweet and beautiful that she will be happy everywhere, everyone will love her, they'll find other parents for her, to replace the dead ones.... And yet I know that no one has entered this block, none of those inside it could have seen her husband, could have given her news. Has she lost her reason also? She has been locked up for three days already....

On the evening of the third day, sometimes the second, again the order is given to us all: *Lagersperre* (absolutely forbidden to leave). We hear the sound of the trucks that enter the *Revier* and the neighboring blocks with the cries *"schnell, rasch, los..."* (quick, fast, out). We hear the cries of the victims who cling with all their meager strength to the doors, to the wheels of the trucks, who call to us for help... the blows rain down on them, and we nurses help them climb into the trucks covered with closed tarps. The ones that can no longer move, the ones dying and the dead, are all thrown on top of each other. They are counted, the missing are found out, the ones who slipped behind the block, clinging to the walls in order not to be seen.

But they will find them all, the number will be complete....

Above the cries a song rises. It's the Jewish anthem, in Greek, and often the Marseillaise also....

"Sing, aren't you going to Palestine?" the *Lagerführerin* (camp commander) shouts ironically at them.

When they've arrived in front of the crematoriums, the sad cargo is unloaded by opening the truck bed. The "work" must be done quickly....

They don't lose much time after that. The sick are already naked, which eliminates the bother of undressing them. They are piled into gas chambers, we still hear a few cries, a few calls for help, a few names, which they shout out at the approach of death, and then, a silence, a profound silence, a silence of death floats over everything....

In the night, huge flames[29] rise up from the chimneys, enormous fat flames, red, which cry out for revenge....

The selections are not made in the *Revier* alone; they are carried out throughout the camp.

The commission goes from one block to the others. All the Jews file in front of it, usually naked. When the commission is in a hurry, the Jews file by fully clothed. A little sign of the hand from the doctor, the number is taken down, the warrant signed. All the women who are thin or who have a bad complexion are taken, or whose rags look more neglected than the others' (for we are given rags, but we must be well dressed), all those who have scabies, a wound, an infirmity in their feet... or, to complete the required number, anyone at all could be taken, it's a question of luck, of chance.

Block 25 in the Birkenau camp[30] is a block for women condemned to death. The "selected" are brought there, locked up, guarded carefully by the S.S. and by the personnel of the block, with the *blocova* at the head, who beats them, deprives them of food, refuses them a little water to drink... This woman will later be arrested (denounced by the detainees) during the Liberation by the Red Army and brought to Russia with her comrades who helped her in her chores, along with a few other detainees in the service of the S.S. who were as monstrous as the S.S. and who have hundreds of victims on their conscience.

In general, in block 25, they waited for the number of the condemned to reach a thousand. They sometimes waited for many days, for the gas chambers could contain a thousand people. "Gas is expensive, it would be a shame to waste it on a small number...."

Along with the selections, they begin to carry out some improvements inside the camp around the months of March and April 1944. Higher orders? Initiative of our head S.S. doctor, Mengele? He is the one whose arrival causes the most horror among us, the one who makes the selections with the most impassivity, the selections that are the most unbearable for us. Mengele would tell us, later on, near the end of the same year: "Why is Radio London talking about my 'selections,' why doesn't it say that I have transformed the house of death into a hospital?" (*Totenhaus* into *Krankenhaus*). Another of those camp paradoxes.

The most energetic struggle against lice and scabies begins. The lice inspections, the delousings are done methodically, without interruption. Everywhere in the camp, signs—A LOUSE IS

DEATH—begin to take on a real form for us, no longer ironic. The quantity of lice diminishes, but lice are still found, they will continue to be found till the end of the existence of this camp (January 18, 1945), but they will only be isolated specimens.

The typhus epidemic comes to an end around March or April. After that, we would have only rare cases. They set up a special service that will only deal with the treatment of scabies (hydrochloric acid, thiosulfuric acid). The treatment is effective, but rather prolonged. They bring Mitigol from Germany, which produces marvelous results. The sick pour in for treatment, 2,000 people a day enter treatment; those with pyodermitis are hospitalized, the others follow a treatment with consultations.

Feverish work on plumbing begins in May. They install toilets, washrooms. The blocks are cleaned, bleached, cement floors are made where there had been only earth.

The sick pour in, despite fear of the selections. But selections are rare in summer. They "liquidate" mostly in spring and fall. Why? The year 1944 is not an exception in this sense. The last selection of the spring takes place in the month of April. They resume only in September, just as frightful, just as pitiless as before.

The work of sanitization lasted all summer and, when it was finished, the Germans "liquidated" the Gypsy camp of Blle,[31] that was 1,000 feet away from our own. In one single night, 4,250 Gypsies were gassed!

That is where they transferred the *Revier*, once again in black, dirty blocks, without water, without plumbing. The invalids of Birkenau were transferred to little camps about a quarter of a mile further away, in unhealthy, dirty blocks....

And Birkenau—beautified, cleaned, sanitized—remained empty.

Why? We could only imagine. We sought the explanation in the approach of the Russians.

They could show them a beautiful, clean camp, they would certainly not tell them that the detainees never profited from the ameliorations and underwent only the inconveniences of the work, dirtiness, noise, dust, transfer of the sick from one block to the other, and thus back to the overcrowding in the bunks....

It was also in the month of May that the Germans decided to "liquidate" the Jews of Hungary. Day and night the trains poured in. The command center[32] that, till then, had taken care of the organization of the belongings of those who arrived, was overwhelmed by work and became insufficient. They opened a new camp.[33] They quickly built wooden barracks next to the crematoriums. A bath house[34] was already there. This new camp was Brezinki,[35] the real camp of extermination, of destruction, of death. 1,200 people would work there day and night, then reinforcements from the Lager would be sent. From 1,000 to 1,500 people would come every day to work there all summer long.

And, on May 16, I was sent to be a doctor at this camp.

Brezinki is made up of about forty barracks and a bath house, all surrounded by electrified barbed wire.

On each side of the barbed wire were the crematoriums[36] (two on one side, three and four on the other), as well as the white house,[37] the gas chamber. Each crematorium also had its own gas chamber.

The tracks[38] were extended from the train station to the crematoriums. That way, they didn't need to use trucks for transportation from the station, and so wasted neither gasoline nor time.

Our work group is made up of just two barracks, surrounded by a wall of barbed wire with a gate that is always locked. Opposite is the "sauna," about 80 feet to the right. Crematoriums 1 and 2 are about 650 feet beyond.[39] A storehouse serves as repository for the belongings of the newcomers who are incarcerated in Auschwitz (all the little camps bearing the names of Birkenau, Brezinki,[40] Auschwitz, Babitz,[41] Buna-Monowitz,[42] Raisko[43] are dependent on Auschwitz and all together form what the world today knows under the name Auschwitz).

I have one room for consultations, and a sick room where I can keep patients for no more than ten days at the most; since our camp is considered a work camp, it is not possible to keep patients longer. We must hurry them to the Birkenau camp.

But we rarely comply with the letter of the law. Besides, what law do we have here but evil treatment, torture, death? Everything we do is nothing but "illegal." So we keep all our patients, except the infectious ones (those with scarlet fever and typhus). I say "we," for in July they sent to Brezinki another woman doctor with whom I would work until the liquidation of the camp, or the evacuation in January 1945, during the lightning advance of the Russians.

It was in Brezinki that I fell into the very heart of hell. Day and night, almost without pause, trains arrived bringing 800,000 Hungarian Jewish women between May and September,[44] a number given to us in the camp by the S.S. who, cynically, always promise us "work" and often announce the transports to us in advance.

Coming in between these Hungarian deliveries, from time to time, a delivery from France, from Belgium, from Holland or Czechoslovakia, Italy or Yugoslavia.... Jewish transports, for the most part.

The trains follow each other almost without pause, unloading onto the road thousands and thousands of people. A quick selection is made by the camp doctor even as the train is unloading. On Sundays, an orchestra plays.

A few young men and women, in good health, are set apart and led to the bath house. They are the "fortunate" ones, the ones chosen for a slave's "existence" with all the wretchedness, hunger, humiliation, and slow death in shameful overcrowding.

The others are led to the gas chambers, the ovens... and, in front of our block, sometimes under the driving rain, sometimes under a burning sun, floods of people pass by, flow by, young women holding children in their arms, women who on the way are still giving their breast full of life, full of sap, to keep their babies from crying.... Their skirts are clutched by the little children who already know how to walk, superb children, brown-haired and blond, with their curls floating on the breeze; the little girls have big bows in their hair.... And young men, able-bodied, strong, the ones who do not want to be separated from their families, who prefer to stay with them in the "work camps," as their fellow citizens in the Germans' pay, who have stayed at home, have solemnly promised them.... And the young women and men who support their exhausted mothers and fathers, sick or bent under the weight of bundles, bags that, when they were disembarking from the train, they didn't want to give to the men (our detainees who work at the train station) who tried to take them, promising they'd find them again in the camp. These are their provisions, changes of clothes for the little ones, a chamber pot for the infant, the saucepan to make him his soup as soon as they arrive, a doll, a toy, these are their poor savings of a whole life....

And old people with white hair who can scarcely drag themselves along and the sick held up by their comrades in misery, by the members of their family, tired, exhausted, already in a hurry to arrive; the dead they have to drag behind them....

The Red Cross van is there, it leads or follows the transport, but it is full; it is bringing the gas for their extermination.

And cries, and insults, blows fall on this living lava that doesn't know how to march in rows of five, and doesn't go fast enough.

Curious, questioning eyes, or eyes full of anguish, lock on us, see the detainees in the window of our block, in the opening of the door; they are the ones who, while the S.S. weren't looking at them, have succeeded in commandeering the openings, for, you never know, there might be that child, or mother, or father, or brother, or sister who stayed hidden at home and who might now be arriving. And often, one of us lets out a cry or falls in a faint. She has seen in the line flowing to the crematorium the ones who are dearest to her in the world, the ones who are her reason for being, the ones who gave her the courage to bear her martyr's life.

And we look on, tense, our teeth clenched in rage; hatred for our executioners makes us tighten our fists, bite our lips.

Should we tell the ones passing by that they are going to their death, that, a few steps further on, it's not a shower as the

S.S. told them and as the inscription at the entrance to the gas chamber promises (*Bade*, bath), but the gas chamber itself... their death. Isn't it better to leave them in ignorance until the last minute? What use would rebellion be? Without weapons, their hands empty, they are defeated in advance. Their action would serve no purpose, their moral and physical torture would only be greater....

And, silent and powerless, we are witnesses to this procession. Our burning gazes follow them to the end.

They make them enter the crematoriums. They tell them to undress for the "shower," to tie their shoes together by the laces so they don't have to search for them on the way out (actually so that they don't get mismatched).

The male detainees who work in the crematoriums help them with blows and shouts. They make them take off their jewelry, their wedding rings, their watches, and they push them into the gas chamber. Now they are beginning to understand....

The gas chamber has two little windows, barred skylights.[45] Hands cling to them, stretch out to the air, we hear children crying, cries of "mama, mama," they call to us for help... and when the room is full (one thousand people in all), two S.S., wearing gas masks, approach the two little windows, pour the gas into them (from cans) and hermetically seal them.... The silence is total. Death takes seven minutes....

The men of the crematorium work group load into vans or handcars all the belongings, suitcases, carefully tied shoes of the gassed. All that will go to our barracks, where our women will sort through them, classify them, and send them to Germany.

After half an hour, everything is finished, clean.

They open the door to the gas chamber.[46] The bodies of the ones who had been close to the door fall out, the others are all lying on top of each other, all on their stomachs, as if all these beings had tried to save themselves from the gas by bending low.... The bodies will be quickly transported to the ovens.... The site is clean, and they can bring in those who were waiting their turn in front of the crematorium.

For, between May and August 1944, the "throng" is so great that the five gas chambers[47] (each one able to accommodate 1,000 people), functioning day and night, are no longer enough. They make people line up in front of the crematoriums, they wait patiently for hours at a time outside, often already undressed, completely naked, they wait for hours on the grass....

And the four chimneys[48] are no longer enough, either. They have huge ravines dug[49] between the crematoriums. Whole work groups do nothing but carry wood to these ravines, they sprinkle the bodies with gasoline... huge red flames rise furiously from the ravines, climb the chimneys.... A terrifying smell of melted fat, charred bones surrounds our camp....

And since there is not, at one point, enough killing gas, they content themselves with just barely asphyxiating people.[50] Cries keep rising up from the flames... and we continue to live!

And, opposite us, in the bath house, another tragedy is being played out.

The doctor comes to inspect the living merchandise, completely naked, he has chosen for the camp! The thin, the sick, and above all pregnant women might have slipped in, without his being aware of it, so gently, politely, he questions the women who seem pregnant or sick to him. He explains to them that it's in their own interest for them to confess to him that they're expecting a child, or that they are tired.... He will give them lighter work, extra food. The women, touched by so much kindness, freely confess. They are set apart, a coat is thrown over their shoulders, a child who could have slipped into the sauna without being seen is placed next to them (the Polish Jewish women knew, for instance, that children were burned, and they sometimes managed to hide them between their legs) and they are brought to the crematorium.

Often, they summon me to the "sauna" to revive a woman in a fainting fit, to remove a needle one of them has tried to embed in a vein (for they separated her from her children, from her mother or from her husband), another tried to cut her veins....

And all these women assail me, question me about their families, their husbands, ask me if the children won't be too unhappy in the "family camps" where they were brought along with an aunt, a grandmother, a member of the family, if they will have the right to see them every day....

It's not worth it to tell them the truth. They will learn soon enough, as soon as they arrive in the camp.

But they are also beginning to understand, they see the flames, they smell the stench....

But can anyone believe in things so monstrous, so inhuman...? When they finally come to know, they still won't believe in them.... And we, who live in the very heart of this hell, we know, we see, but do we truly realize what we are seeing?

How can we continue to live after this? It is only hatred that gives us strength, and hope to see the Nazi regime collapse before our own eyes, the hope that one day we will help the living world prevent the return of these crimes!

And while they are gassing, while they are burning, while they are fashioning female slaves who will enter the camp, having chosen them for life and suffering (they have shaved them, dressed them in rags, searched them so they have nothing left, not even a worthless souvenir, tattooed them after separating them from the people who had been closest to them and who were their reason for existence), our group works and eats.

I say the group "works"—for the last belongings, clothes, bags, packages that the new arrivals still had with them when they came to the sauna have to be gathered together, placed in the bins where other detainees classify them (jewelry, money, medicine, men's clothing, women's clothing, underwear, blankets, dishes, rugs, new cloth, curtains, food, toys... each article in a special bin). They are brushed and cleaned; articles of the same kind are made up into packages to be loaded onto trucks that take them to the train station and, from there, to Germany. The rags are kept for the camp detainees.

I say the group "eats"—for the newcomers were carrying food, and we are hungry. Shopping bags, packages are searched. A piece of chocolate, a cake, a piece of sausage, jam and lard are quickly devoured, a can of sardines or pickles, a piece of bread are quickly hidden in trousers (the detainees in Brezinki worked wearing pants), or in a shirt, even at the risk of having our hair cut if there is a search. And yet, we are often searched.

And after twelve hours of work (there is a day team and a night team) these girls, having returned to the block, give themselves veritable orgies of food. What does it matter to them that the flames are rising to the sky, that the stench of scorched bones tightens the throat, that one hears cries and shouts for help coming from the flames, that our sisters in misery are writhing in pain in the sauna, since the flesh of their flesh has just been torn from them, their children, their mother, their husband, what does it matter that they are already hungry and cold. They eat gluttonously, the fat runs down their fingers, onto the beds, they gossip, they laugh.... No writer, no poet could ever describe this life. Is this what hell is?

The world of the living—for we, we are dead people, since we are certain of never leaving—will it someday know what happened in this little forest (the Brezinki camp), and will it know how to draw conclusions from it?

And the ovens work without pause. Their living fuel is provided to them regularly.

When the majority of the Hungarian transports was done, they began to liquidate the rest of the Polish ghettos. Last September, 80,000 Jews, all of them from Lodz, went to the ovens, as well as those from Radom, and the last remaining ones from Lublin, and thousands and thousands of others....

And as the Russians advanced, tens of thousands of Jews from all over Europe are brought. Foreseeing their defeat, the S.S. still take vengeance on women, on children without weapons, without defense, without protection; they are "saving" Europe from the Jewish threat!

We will see tens of thousands of Jews from Theresienstadt (Czechoslovakia) pass by, as well as Slovaks and, sometimes, not so often, a Dutch transport. The last transport from France took place in the beginning of September, from

the Montluc prison. This is a surprise for the Auschwitz author-
ities, since they weren't expecting any more transports from
France. The French prisoners would stay for ten days in one of
the barracks, without eating (we helped them by sending them a
part of what we got for ourselves, by stealing a few provisions
from the German women), waiting for an answer from Berlin to
find out what should be done with them. A few died while waiting. The answer is favorable for them, however. They will not be
gassed. They are all made to return to the camp.

However, in between the Jewish transports, "Aryan"
transports arrive who, like us, are undressed, tattooed, shaved
when lice are found on them, dressed in rags, and sent to the
camp. There, their life will be as hard as our own, but they
will have a right to letters and packages. The largest of these
transports came from Poland. A part of the free population
of Warsaw was sent to Auschwitz during the revolt of
September 1944.

The work camp and the family camp that German
propaganda had promised them was actually the hard labor
camp of Auschwitz!

But in September 1944 the threat of the Russian advance
on our camp becomes more pressing. They decide on a
gradual evacuation of this camp, on a liquidation of
Auschwitz. And the word "liquidation" in the Germans' mouth
takes on a precise form for us....

They begin with the Gypsy camp. Four thousand two hundred fifty "Tziganes," men, women, and children, are led to the crematorium ovens and gassed in one night. And they knew where they were being led; they fought, they cried, they shouted out, the children called for their mothers in every language (once I met, by chance, in a Gypsy work group which I was searching for lice and scabies, Frenchwomen who were born in France, of French parents, who didn't know any other language but French, and who had been gathered together in France and sent to this Gypsy camp simply because they were fairground peddlers), they called to us for help....

The next day, long red flames will no longer call for help, but for revenge this time.

And on this same day, the order is given to the secretariat to make them all dead, exterminate them, since the camp has been, in their words, "contaminated" by syphilis....

Every night, the headlights from the trucks going to the crematorium ovens light up our windows. We count them during sleepless nights to know how many of our brothers and sisters died that night.

The S.S. doctor from the camp "will work hard," he will make selections without stopping.

And, from time to time, little transports leave by train, 100, 300, or 500 people, in an unknown direction. Is it for life or for death? We hear cries and calls for help all night long....

An S.S. woman, when I naively remarked that it would take a long time to evacuate such a camp, said to me cynically, "No, very quickly—at least 75% will go to the *Himmelkommando* (the work group in the sky)."

Around the end of November,[51]a new sensational piece of information passes from mouth to mouth: the Germans will stop gassing and burning! Is this one of the many false rumors circulating in the camp? One day they say a commission from the international Red Cross is supposed to visit the camp, another day that the Wehrmacht (the army) is going to take over command of the camp and replace the S.S. We cling all the same to this hope, we want to believe it.

In fact, from that moment, the transports to Auschwitz were rare, and there were no more selections within the camp. From time to time, a little transport left in an unknown direction; with heavy hearts, we would wonder to what new crematorium it had been sent. And the "well-informed" people told us that 50 miles from us they had built modern crematorium ovens where everything worked on electricity....

Is it true, did the S.S. start this rumor to torture us morally a little more? Impossible to make them talk about it, they are "mute."

But why not believe it? Haven't we already seen entire transports come from other camps and be sent directly to the gas chambers? They were usually transports of tired, worn-out people, from whom all their strength for work had already been drawn ("Mussulmen," we called them, beings reduced to the state of zombies). One day we saw a transport arrive at our place, with 500 children between ten and fourteen years old, still healthy children, children of the Gypsies they said, coming from Dachau. They were gassed in our camp as soon as they arrived.

In Brezinki, the work continues, feverishly. The barracks are full to overflowing. As quickly as possible, we must classify, clean, make packages, send to Germany the goods confiscated, stolen, from the whole world.

At the end of November, everyone must classify the clothes of children, and children's toys.... Urgent orders from Berlin, the S.S. tell us. We know that Christmas is approaching, that gifts for German children must be made. And the clothes and toys of hundreds of little children burnt alive will make the eyes of the children of the S.S. gleam with joy....

And our women work day and night, these things burning their hands, and the trains follow each other, trains loaded with toys, with children's underwear and clothing, with blankets, curtains, precious rugs, shoes, dishes, new cloth, boxes of gold, of jewels, of bank notes from various countries....

And when the yield isn't good, the S.S. come for "sport" on Sunday with our women already exhausted from work (for there is a half-day free on Sunday and every two weeks).

"Sport" means that under the orders of an S.S. officer, brandishing a big, heavy stone, they have to walk, run, throw themselves on the ground, get up, jump, crawl on their knees, get up again... without stopping, without interruption for an hour, an hour and a half, two hours. Blows rain down on the ones who can no longer keep up with the others. And we are in a region that is covered in mud almost all year long. Dirty as pigs, exhausted, dead with fatigue, we return to the block in the evening. And, next morning, work begins again....

On the morning of January 18th, there's a rumor that the camp is going to be evacuated. The kitchen is no longer functioning; our soup wasn't brought to us at noon. Feverishly, the S.S. are burning the official documents, the account books of the different centers, our registration slips, etc. A large bonfire where they burn empty suitcases....

At five p.m., we receive the order to line up, without delay, in order to leave. They allow us to bring a blanket and whatever else we want. In the barracks, the merchandise is guarded by the S.S., but we still try at the last minute to get one more sweater, a change of shirts for ourselves.

The S.S., weapons in hand, search the blocks to see if anyone has stayed behind. But no one dares hide themselves in the barracks for we've known for a long time that they would blow up Brezinki. And, in fact, after our departure, the barracks were set on fire. They couldn't let the enemy find proofs of their crimes....

At six o'clock, our column gets underway and starts marching. We don't dare believe we are leaving Brezinki, that they didn't gas all of us, that we are leaving alive. And, in weather that's 15 below, we walk cheerfully, quickly, we leave behind us this cursed land where millions of people lost their lives, more than 4 million according to the statistics,[52] where each one of us has left someone close to us, a parent, a child, a friend....

The fires lit everywhere illuminate the night. They burn, they erase the traces of Nazi crimes....

But, even if we are walking toward new crematorium ovens as we imagine, and as they say, we are certain now that some of us will still escape, and that the world will learn, despite everything, what AUSCHWITZ was! What does it matter that we die on the way, or at the finish.

The end of the Nazi regime is near, the world will know everything, the world will take revenge!

We pass in front of all the little camps of Auschwitz. Everything is empty, everywhere fires are burning. And, on the way, we meet other columns of evacuees from Auschwitz, endless columns of women and men, people in rags, scarcely clothed, sick people, beaten out of the hospitals and infirmaries with clubs at the last minute.

The S.S. shove us, order us to walk faster. A north wind is blowing. Our hands and feet are freezing. We get rid of the little packages we brought with us (things we had taken from the camp stores at the last minute), just throwing them on the road. We wrap ourselves up in our blankets, support each other and... we march forward. A wonderful night, a road all covered in snow, little woods on each side of the road.

We could perhaps, without the S.S. seeing us, slip quietly into this little wood and wait for the arrival of the Russians there. But we only have our coats, our dresses with the crosses painted on the backs, we are tattooed and penniless. We don't know the countryside, and, above all, the language. And the Polish women, we've gotten to know them in the camp! It's not the inhabitants of Poland who will help us in our flight. The first one who sees us would certainly take pleasure in turning us in. We've had proof of this, moreover. At nightfall, one of my Slovak colleagues, on the road, had spoken to a Polish woman who was passing us and, since she had asked her if we were far from the Czech border (we almost passed alongside it), the woman replied that she would bring her husband to her who would show her the way.... And, a few minutes later, she saw this same woman come towards us with an S.S. officer and, from far away, point out my colleague to him, easily recognizable because of her white scarf. Quickly, she took off her scarf and slipped into the ranks. This Polish woman was no better than the one we had known in camp.

And fatigue began to overtake us. Around midnight, we began to see the corpses of our detainees stretched out in the snow, with a bullet in the head, sometimes in the stomach.... They are the ones who, having left before us, couldn't go any further and were shot down on the way. From time to time, a shot ringing out behind or in front of us lets us know that another one of our own had fallen....

For we didn't have the right to pause, to drop to the back, to sit down a little on the edge of the road. The S.S. had orders to shoot at anyone who couldn't follow. We no longer talk to each other, we no longer sing. Like automatons we keep pressing forward.

We have walked for fourteen hours without stopping, without having a minute of rest. We have only covered 25 miles. The next morning, we have our first pause at 8 in the morning at a public square, in a Polish village, in front of a school. Many of us are missing. Shot along the road, escaped into the woods? We would like to think so, but we have heard too many gunshots in the night....

We sit down in the snow. We eat a heel of dry, frozen bread with a little margarine (less than an ounce), we suck on a little clean snow.

After two hours, we again have to line up in rows of five and press on. But we are walking poorly, we drag ourselves lamentably along the road and, a few miles further on, they bring us to a stable. A few cows are still there, it smells bad but there is a little straw. We throw ourselves on this straw that seems to us as soft as the finest beds, we pile on top of each other, for there are 2,000 of us in one single stable, and we sleep a dreamless sleep.

We won't leave there till the next morning, as stiff and tired as the day before. On the second day, we cover another 20 miles and, in the evening, we arrive in Loslau where cattle cars with open gates are waiting for us.

With gunshots and blows from clubs, the S.S. load us up, 100 in each car, and leave us on the track, while they go into the waiting room of the train station or under the archways to warm themselves next to lighted fires. It is −26 degrees Fahrenheit that night, they say....

In vain do we press against each other, it is terribly cold, we can hardly inhale. In the middle of the night, we fled the cars and took refuge in the station toilets where, standing up, splashing in the water, we could wash ourselves and warm up a little.

Early in the morning, the S.S. noticed our flight and again loaded us into the same open cars, where we spent another entire day. At night, our train left and we rode in the same cars for five days, still without eating. Fortunately there was snow, and during the stops we could get a little clean snow for ourselves. Our bread and our meager provisions had been finished long ago.

The women who died on the way were unloaded onto the road and left there. No one knew either their names, or even their numbers....

On January 25th, we arrived in Ravensbrück, happy to be anywhere and no longer in the open cars where we had stayed crouching, no longer able even to sit down, since there was no room!

But in Ravensbrück, there was no more room for us. To begin with, they brought us to the Jugendlager where we were piled into an empty block, 2,000 of us, still on the ground, still sitting.

The day after our arrival, they handed out soup to us. I received a thermos cup, which I shared with a sick comrade who couldn't go out and fight for her soup. They gave us a fifth of a loaf of bread, and it was still snow that completed our meal!

At dawn, we go out through the windows (impossible to reach the door over the bodies) and we wash ourselves, also with snow. The cold has become less intense and, one fine morning, it's a catastrophe, the snow has melted... Moreover it had been so dirty the last few days that we could no longer use it for eating, but we could at least wash ourselves with it. This time, we wash ourselves in cisterns filled with dirty water....

A few days after our arrival, we try to ask for a little more soup. The *Oberführerin* (the chief S.S.) of the camp arrives; she announces to us in a stentorian voice that we must have forgotten that we had no right to live, and consequently, we would be deprived of food—for three days. Our fifth of bread is still distributed to us, though, but nothing along with it (margarine or cheese), and no soup. A few detainees can no longer move, and fall unconscious. What can we do? If we had a piece of bread to give them, their illness might pass....

With a group of doctors and nurses from Auschwitz, we occupy a corner of the barracks. The sick arrive. But we have no more medicine, no more bandages. And the ones who have frozen feet and gangrene, dysentery or typhoid, erysipelas, press around us. We can't even provide them with a little room for them to lie down.

And when I manage to ask the *Oberschwester* (head nurse) for at least a few aspirin tablets, a few bandages, or the right to bring the sick people to the hospital, she replies: "Aren't you Jewish? You forget that you have no right to live!"—the leitmotif in Ravensbrück.

Every morning, the dead are brought out into the courtyard.

After ten days of this life of hell, they finally bring us to the camp, where we at least regularly get our ration of bread, and theoretically our one-third of a liter of soup, since they only give us one liter for three people.

But everyone doesn't have this luck. Some sleep in the camp beneath tents, on the ground, in the mud. Every day, little transports leave for other camps.

Our turn arrives on February 14th. At night, they put us in cars where we stand or sit on the floor and, after a night of traveling, we arrive in Neustadt Gleve in Mecklenburg, but Neustadt can no longer receive us, since there's no more room. It's a little camp, made for 800 to 900 women who work in the aviation factory; already, the day before, another transport of 1,700 had arrived.

We spend all day on the platforms, still without anything to eat and, at night, they bring us to a barn where there is a little straw near the aviation factory. There are 1,600 of us piled together. They make us go in like cattle into a stable; the S.S. push us with help of their batons and their leather belts. They are aided in their work by German prisoners, who exhibit as much zeal as the S.S.

Aren't we in Germany, where the word "Jew" is thrown at our faces like the greatest insult, at each instant, and where they keep saying that we have no right to live?

The German and Polish women detainees seize the occasion to show their hatred of the Jews by beating us, bullying us at every opportunity. They begin by spreading out their blankets in the barn and lying on top of them, while we have only the right to remain seated or standing; woe betide anyone who brushes against one of these "ladies" while passing by....

Every day, we stand outside for hours at roll-call and, after roll-call, they distribute our bread to us, the ration already diminished to a sixth. After the third day we're given a little soup, three or four spoonfuls per person. But each time after this distribution and this roll-call, we have to return to the barn under blows that rain down and, inside, more blows await us, from the Polish and German women defending their places. We are beaten to make us leave the barn, beaten to make us return to it, beaten to go to the toilet (no water this whole time), beaten for having moved a little.

After ten days, we are led to the camp. They have emptied the barracks that had been occupied by civilian émigrés and we are put there in their place.

Our entry to the camp began with a strict search, made by the woman director of the camp (a German criminal who was there for having killed her husband and child) and S.S. women, in the presence of the camp commander. They took away our blankets, our change of underwear, left us only one single pullover, and sent us into our respective blocks. The blocks were divided into little rooms by wooden dividers; there were 90 of us in our room (13 X 14 feet), sitting on the ground on a little straw. Over the windows, barbed wire.

Every night the quarrels begin, for we cannot lie down. We have to lie on top of each other, we can't turn over at night unless our neighbor turns over; everyone suspects her neighbor of taking one centimeter more than she had the day before, of being too comfortable. Impossible to wash. There is one toilet, but we can only go to it at certain times of the day (impossible to know when in advance), and it's only the friends of the Polish and German women who can enter it; the others get beaten over the head with batons. The same is true for the washrooms. And, every day, there are at least two or three women who are beaten by our detainee "directors." Useless to lodge a complaint, the others are friends of the S.S., of the Germans, they will always be judged in the right....

Food is almost nonexistent. Until April, we regularly got eight ounces of soup at most, sometimes just two spoonfuls of soup—"soup" is lukewarm, unsalted water, with a few slices of turnips floating in it sometimes—and a sixth of a loaf of bread. In April they increased our ration of soup (the quality remained the same), but we get only a tenth of bread, 5 ounces a day of a heavy bread, two little slices in all. Everything comes at once. So we eat once a day, around 4 or 5 o'clock, and wait for the next day, our stomachs hollow.

No one, or almost no one, worked. A few small work groups went out into the woods to dig trenches. They only rarely took a few girls to unload potatoes or turnips at the train station. And these jobs were highly sought out, for one could eat on site, and, at the risk of losing one's hair, one could bring into the block a few raw potatoes or a piece of turnip... and these things are considered delicacies... I remember wondering, quite seriously, if when I got home I would also eat raw potatoes!

In Neustadt, Jewish women did not have the right to occupy posts in the hospital, so I worked only unofficially, especially doing prophylactic sanitary work in the block, keeping scabies and lice under control. We were all covered with them, and we had to force the detainees to kill them by searching underwear and clothing as often as possible.

I managed to find a few medicines and bandages at the hospital. I brought my sickest patients there, but generally they would accept only the dying, since places were limited and there were many patients.

Every day, at roll-call, during which we had to remain standing as always, many of us fell in a faint. When the directors turned away, we sat down on the ground, since no one could remain standing any longer. And dysentery, tuberculosis, swelling from malnutrition wrought terrible damage. Most of the detainees had ulcerating stomatitis. The women changed as we watched, literally melted away, had that sallow complexion, that wrinkled, yellow skin, of camp inmates.

Rumors of the Allied advance reached us. We knew liberation was near, but we also knew that for us, each day, each hour cost many lives....

And on May 1st* secretly, there was a celebration in the camp. We spread out on a piece of cotton cellulose our slices of bread, shared by everyone, which we had garnished with slices of raw potatoes and raw beets, "organized" the day before by one of our girls who helped unload a train car. Then we sang.

On the morning of May 3rd, the S.S. locked us up in our barracks. No group left to work outside. From our windows, we had seen the S.S. taking out provisions from our camp store (warehouse). A few of us managed to break the barbed wire and at around two in the afternoon, the first of us escaped. At the same time, we heard a shout, American tanks were passing in front of the camp....

Then the S.S. abandoned their suitcases, the loaded trucks, and escaped with their girlfriends, our German detainees, shooting at our women who had escaped from the block before leaving. Some were wounded, many seriously. But the American tanks were only passing by and were going to occupy the train station. We were free and alone....

The crowd of our freed detainees threw themselves on the store of provisions, on the suitcases and things abandoned by the S.S. in their flight. Terrible scenes took place. People fought each

*May 1st was the date that year of the Jewish festival of Lag B'Omer—Trans.

other, killed each other to snatch at the bread or the package of margarine or the few raw potatoes that the strongest had succeeded in obtaining. After half an hour not one provision was left in the camp. And the weak and sick looked at us anxiously, asking us if we could give them at least their ration of bread. But the storehouse was empty, and the Americans had only passed by.

Around the end of the day, a few Americans appeared in front of the camp. We called to them, showed them our sick, asked them to help us. They sent us to their commander. And the next day, the commander told us he could do nothing for us. He promised to see us later on....

In the afternoon, the Russian troops arrived... and two days later we had been transferred, through their efforts, to the city itself, to the German military hospital, abandoned by the German doctors and the lightly wounded. The Russians placed at our disposal the German staff, who did the hardest work, and also pharmaceutical products. They supplied us wonderfully with provisions—milk, butter, meat every day, potatoes, sugar. They dressed us, gave us cloth and seamstresses to make clothes for our patients. They gave us leather and shoemakers to have sandals made for us.

And seven weeks later, most of our patients, having regained their strength, could be repatriated in normal condition. The others—the very ill, those with incurable diseases—were sent back in ambulances.

ENDNOTES

[1] Arthur Koestler, *Scum of the Earth*. New York: Macmillan, 1941 (about Le Vernet).

[2] Lion Feuchtwanger, *The Devil in France*. New York: Viking, 1941 (about Les Milles).

[3] Jean-Jacques Bernard, *Le Camp de la mort lente* (The camp of slow death). Paris: Albin Michel, 1944 (about Compiègne).

[4] Roger Gompel, *Pour que tu ne m'oublies pas* (So that you won't forget me), diary published in 1980 (about Compiègne and Drancy).

[5] Nissim Calef, *Drancy, Campo di Rappresaglie*. Edizione Italiana, 1945. Published in French as *Drancy 1941:*

Camp de représailles, Drancy la faim. Paris: FFDJF ("Les fils et filles des déportés juifs de France"), 1991.

[6] Georges Wellers, *De Drancy à Auschwitz*. Paris: Editions du Centre, 1946. *Un Juif sous Vichy*, Paris: Editions Tirésias, 1991.

[7] Georges Kohn, *Journal de Compiègne et de Drancy*. Paris: FFDJF, 1999.

[8] David Olère, *L'Oeil du témoin* (The eye of the witness). Paris: Editions Klarsfield, 1988. Translated into English as *Witness: Images of Auschwitz*, N. Richland Hills, Texas: WestWind Press, 1998.

[9] Serge Miller, *Le Laminoir* (The steamroller). Paris: Calmann-Lévy, 1947.

[10] *Le Monde juif*, October-December issue, 1990. NI 140.

[11] Jean-Claude Pressac, *Auschwitz: Technique and Operation of the Gas Chambers*. New York: The Beate Klarsfeld Foundation, 1989.

[12] "Sima Vaisman's testimony is published completely, just as written in 1945, without any changes."—From the editors of *Le Monde juif*, 1945.

[13] Transport No. 66, which left the Drancy camp on January 20, 1944. It transported 1,155 deported Jews, 640 men and 515 women. Of the deportees, 221 were younger than eighteen, and included 3 babies born in 1943, 5 in 1942, and 8 in 1941.

A survivor of Convoy 66, Suzanne Birnbaum, described her deportation immediately upon returning in *Une Française juive est revenue* (A Jewish Frenchwoman has returned), Paris: Le Livre français, 1945.

[14] The convoy arrived at the Auschwitz train station on the night of January 22. The men were selected before midnight (on the 22nd), the women after midnight (on the 23rd). After selection, 236 men numbered from 172,611 to 172,846 and 55 women numbered from 74,783 to 74,797 and from 74,835 to 74,874 were declared "able-bodied." The rest of the convoy, 864 people, were gassed in Crematorium II or III. In 1945, there were 72 survivors of this convoy, including 30 women.

[15] The unloading of the trains, and then the selection, took place at that time on the "old Jewish ramp," one kilometer south of the Auschwitz train station, alongside the tracks.

[16] Probably one of the two "Bauwerk (Worksites)" 5a and 6b. These facilities made it possible to delouse clothing with Zyklon-B (hydrocyanic acid) in gas chambers built for this purpose and to destroy parasites in autoclaves or hot-air chambers. They had also been equipped with a room of 50 communal showers and with an actual sauna—hence the name given by the author, the "Zentral Sauna," being a "sauna" in name only, since it now was without a

sauna. This sanitary facility was comprised of 3 "Goedecker" autoclaves, 4 "Topf" hot-air chambers, and 50 communal showers.

[17] These barracks, called "permanent" to differentiate them from "the stables" put up later on, were built with bricks that came from the demolition of some neighborhoods of the city of Oswiecim and were set up in the first construction block of K.G.L. Birkenau, the B.A.I. The author was "penned" in the BIb sector, called the "Women's Camp."

[18] This rumor is unfounded.

[19] *Stubovas, blocovas*: this mixture of Polish and German, which became the camp slang, is a good illustration of the spheres of influence in the camp: the words have German roots from which they derive their meaning, but are completely engulfed by the Polish environment.

[20] "Two faucets": not for the entire camp, but for the sector where the author was "accommodated."

[21] The BIIf sector (see map) was the camp hospital. It was made up of eighteen wooden barracks, most of them "stables."

[22] From its creation (July 1940) until its liberation, the Auschwitz camp suffered over a dozen typhus epidemics. They were either widespread (ravaging the entire

complex, as in August 1942), or confined to a sector or a camp (the case for the Gypsy camp or sector BIIe around mid-June 1942).

[23] See on the map the position of Barrack 18 in sector BIIf.

[24] In July 1944, K.G.L. Birkenau held 60,000 detainees, men and women.

[25] Names of medications cited by the author:

—charcoal: anti-diarrheal;

—urotropine: internal antiseptic used for infections of the urinary and biliary canals, anti-infection;

—Tamalbrul: probably a product like Tannalbin (a combination of tannin and albumen) or tanacetyl (acetyltanin) or tannoform. All these products are anti-diarrheal;

—cardiozol: respiratory and cardiovascular stimulant;

—caffeine: tonic for the heart as well as a diuretic;

—Prontosil: chlorydrate of sulfamidochrysoidine. One of the first sulfa drugs to be used. Anti-microbial action;

—kaolin: absorbent for ulcers. Used in dermatology;

—Solvens: sodium sulforicinate also sold under the names Solvise and Polysolve. This syrupy liquid, dark yellow, when emulsified with water, was used in laryngeal tuberculosis.

[26] The delousing of personal effects in the buildings designed for this purpose began, in fact, at the end of 1943: the

Entwesunganlager [Disinfection Installations] (Bw 5a and 5b) of B.A.I. were completed on October 26, 1943, the "Zentral Sauna" was finished on January 29, 1944, and the Entwesungsbaracke [Disinfection Barrack] in the Gypsy camp was completed on February 17, 1944.

[27] At that time, to the "Zentral Sauna," which was comprised of two large heated waiting rooms with a cement floor (one for the *unreine*, or dirty, side, and one for the *reine*, or clean, side).

[28] Dark purple crystals used as in Dakin's solution; a disinfectant.

[29] All you had to do was leave Block 18 and walk about three hundred feet south along the barbed wire fence to see the crematoriums, visible only from the outside, because of the flames the two chimneys (one per crematorium) spat out. Crematoriums IV and V, on the other hand, were not visible from the camp hospital.

[30] It is impossible to locate this block, since there were six blocks bearing the number "25" in all of K.G.L. Birkenau.

[31] According to the documents preserved, from February 26, 1943, to July 21, 1944, a little fewer than 22,000 Gypsies (men, women, and children) were "concentrated" in Birkenau, in sector BIIe, called the "Gypsy Camp" (*Zigeunerfamilienlager*). On August 2, 1944, the survivors, about 3,000 altogether, were gassed.

[32] The author is referring to the men and women detainees working in Canada I, set up in the first industrial zone in the camp, between the main camp and the train station.

[33] This refers to Canada II, situated west of the second construction block (BII) in Birkenau. This sector, sometimes called BIIg, was made up of thirty barracks (arranged in three rows of ten), most of them "stables," a few of a different model (with lateral windows).

[34] "Bath house": here the "Zentral Sauna."

[35] "Brezinki": actually Brzezinka, the Polish name for Birkenau. The juxtaposition of many closed spaces surrounded with barbed wire in K.G.L. Birkenau, such as BIa, BIb, BIIa, BIIb, BIIe, BIId, BIIf, Canada II, the yard of crematorium II, and of IV and V, gave the detainees the impression of many separate camps, which could seem true but was administratively false since all these different sectors are K.G.L. Birkenau. When the author cites "Brezinki," the reader should take this to mean Canada II or sector BIIg.

[36] Crematoriums II and III were in the southern part of Canada II; IV and V were in the northern part.

[37] This is Bunker 2, 980 feet west of the Zentral Sauna, made active again in the summer of 1944 under the name Bunker 5 (crematoriums II, III, IV, and V were then called I, II, III, and IV).

38 The construction of three railroad tracks in May 1944 for
   the deportation of Hungarians gave concrete expression
   to an old plan represented in the second map for the
   Birkenau prisoner of war camp, drawn up on October
   14, 1941, and intended for the Soviets. On this map,
   which did not have a crematorium, the railroad line was
   conceived as having two tracks (in and out).

39 The two hospital-barracks of Canada II were 65 feet away
   from the Zentral Sauna (to the west), 160 feet from crematorium IV, 550 feet from crematorium V (in the north),
   1500 feet from crematorium III and 2,000 feet from crematorium II (to the southwest).

40 "Birkenau, Brezinki": these are respectively the German
   and Polish names for the camp.

41 A subsidiary camp situated in the north, about two miles
   from the main Auschwitz camp.

42 The "work camp" of Monowitz is also called "Buna-Monowitz."
   "Buna" designates the I.G. Farben factory meant to
   produce synthetic rubber (by means of the Butadiene-
   Sodium [Na] and methanol [used as fuel] procedure).

43 Rajsko, a locality situated 1.6 miles south of the main
   camp, included the S.S. institute of hygiene and an
   experimental station for the culture of plants (culture of a
   variety of dandelion, the *Taraxacum bicorne*, also called

Kok-saghyz, the roots of which contained 1.5% latex).

[44] From May 17, 1944, to July 11, 1944, a total of 437,402 Jews were deported from Hungary, according to the detailed report of Veesenmayer, German ambassador to Budapest. (See the article by Georges Wellers, "Essai de détermination du nombre de morts au camp d'Auschwitz" [An attempt to determine the number of dead in the Auschwitz camp], in *Le Monde juif* No. 112, 1983.)

[45] The gas chamber which is actually in the block of three gas chambers of crematorium IV (165 feet from the hospital-barracks of Canada II). The witness had a direct and complete view onto the southern façade of the building. In the block of the three gas chambers of crematorium IV, the one to the south had two leak-proof doors (one inner and one outer) with two leak-proof windows for the pouring in of Zyklon-B. This is the first time a visual witness mentions the fact that these openings were equipped with inner bars, probably set back in order to facilitate the flow of the Zyklon-B granules into the room. The presence of two S.S. simultaneously pouring Zyklon-B into one single gas chamber had never before been pointed out.

[46] Usually, the outer doors to the gas chambers of crematoriums IV and V were opened only to allow natural aeration.

The bodies were not taken outside, but transported inside to the central morgue to be stored there before cremation.

[47] There was one gas chamber in crematorium II, one in crematorium III, three in crematorium IV, three, then four, in crematorium V, and four, then—once the inner barriers are built—one more in bunker 2/V.

[48] The author is thinking of the four crematoriums as each having its own chimney. In fact, crematoriums I and III had one chimney each and crematoriums IV and V two chimneys each. When writing "four chimneys," she is directly transposing what she saw every day, the four chimneys of crematoriums IV and V.

[49] When the incineration oven of crematorium V had broken down, the S.S. had five small incineration ditches dug in the northwest courtyard of the building. Starting in July '44, a ten-foot-high hedge was set around crematorium V in order to hide these incineration ditches from the sight of the newcomers.

[50] At the end of the summer of '44, Zyklon-B began to be scarce, because of the growing disorganization of the economy and the transports of the Third Reich. The victims were pushed directly, still living, into the incineration ditches of crematorium V and of bunker 2/V.

51 The order was to dismantle crematoriums II and III, or the
    two main exterminating complexes in Birkenau, housing
    under one roof the homicidal gas chambers and an
    incineration oven. Since crematorium IV had been com-
    pletely taken down in October 1944 following the revolt
    of the Sonderkommando, only the oven of crematorium
    IV continued to function until the evacuation of the camp,
    incinerating the corpses of those who died "naturally."
    This order was given on November 26, 1944.

53 This number is the one asserted by the Soviet and Polish
    commissions. Detailed studies, such as the one by
    George Wellers cited above, have determined the num-
    ber of dead in Auschwitz to be 1,471,595 people,
    1,352,980 of whom were Jewish.

AUSCHWITZ (BIRKENAU) CONCENTRATION CAMP

━■━ Barbed wire	(e) "Sauna"
◄━━► Extension of "Mexico" camp	(f) Mass graves for Russian prisoners
■ Watchtower	(g) Execution site (section of camp B IId)
⋮⋮⋮ Mass graves	(h) Delousing barracks
▬ Cremation pit	(i) Kitchen barracks
(a) Guardroom and gate	Latrines and laundry /cleaning barracks
(b) Command center of Birkenau and S.S. Housing	(30) Block 30, the experimentation block of Dr.Schumann (section of camp B Ia)
(c) Storage camp for things from "Canada"	
(d) Railroad ramp (after May 1944, selections took place here)	

CENTRAL SAUNA
(e)

WATER PURIFICATION BUILDING

GAS CHAMBER AND CREMATORIUM 2

GAS CHAMBER AND CREMATORIUM 3

(c)

STOREHOUSE CAMP FOR THINGS FROM "CANADA"

WATER PURIFICATION BUILDING

B Ib

B I

CENTRAL HOSPITAL

B II

DISINFECTION BUILDING   **B IIf**

22, 24, 26, 28, 30, 32 waren Krankenbau Blöcke

GYPSY CAMP

MEN'S CAMP

HUNGARIAN CAMP

THERESIENSTADT CAMP

B Ia

(30)   (a)

QUARANTINE CAMP

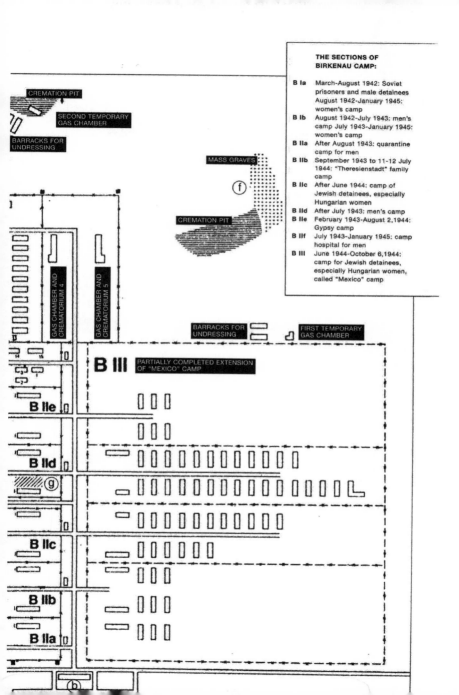

CREMATION PIT

SECOND TEMPORARY
GAS CHAMBER

BARRACKS FOR
UNDRESSING

MASS GRAVES

(f)

CREMATION PIT

**THE SECTIONS OF
BIRKENAU CAMP:**

B Ia   March-August 1942: Soviet
       prisoners and male detainees
       August 1942-January 1945:
       women's camp
B Ib   August 1942-July 1943: men's
       camp July 1943-January 1945:
       women's camp
B IIa After August 1943: quarantine
       camp for men
B IIb September 1943 to 11-12 July
       1944: "Theresienstadt" family
       camp
B IIc After June 1944: camp of
       Jewish detainees, especially
       Hungarian women
B IId After July 1943: men's camp
B IIe February 1943-August 2,1944:
       Gypsy camp
B IIf July 1943-January 1945: camp
       hospital for men
B III June 1944-October 6,1944:
       camp for Jewish detainees,
       especially Hungarian women,
       called "Mexico" camp

GAS CHAMBER AND CREMATORIUM 4

GAS CHAMBER AND CREMATORIUM 5

BARRACKS FOR
UNDRESSING

FIRST TEMPORARY
GAS CHAMBER

B III   PARTIALLY COMPLETED EXTENSION
            OF "MEXICO" CAMP

B IIe

B IId

(g)

B IIc

B IIb

B IIa

(b)

(DETAIL)

GAS CHAMBER AND
CREMATORIUM 2

GAS CHAMBER AND
CREMATORIUM 3

25 26 27

19 20 21

13 14 15

8 9

2 3

22 23 24

16 17 18

10 11 12

4 5 6

B II CENTRAL HOSPITAL

B IIf

L L   32 30 28 26 24 22

22, 24, 26, 28, 30, 32 blocs pou

L L   31 29 27 25 23 21

L L   32 30 28 26 24 22

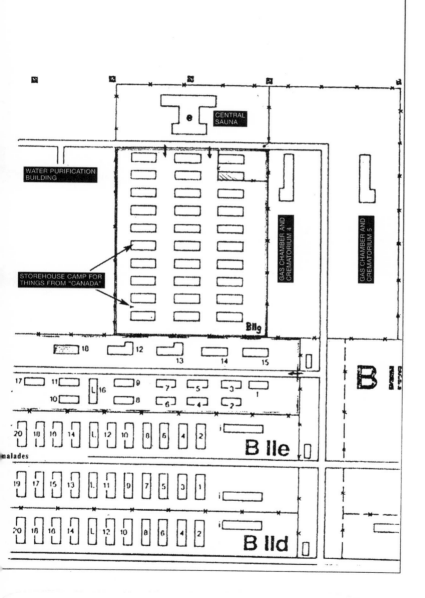

CENTRAL SAUNA

WATER PURIFICATION BUILDING

GAS CHAMBER AND CREMATORIUM 4

GAS CHAMBER AND CREMATORIUM 5

STOREHOUSE CAMP FOR THINGS FROM "CANADA"

B IIg

B II

10   12
        13   14   15

17   11   9   7   5   3   1
      16
10   8   6   4   2

20 18 16 14 L 12 10 8 6 4 2   i

malades

B IIe

19 17 15 13 L 11 9 7 5 3 1   i

20 18 16 14 L 12 10 8 6 4 2   i

B IId